THE OFFICIAL
HIBERNIAN
Football Club
Annual 2017

Written by David Forsyth
Designed by Jon Dalrymple

A Grange Publication

©2016. Published by Grange Communications Ltd., Edinburgh, under licence from Hibernian Football Club. Printed in the EU.

Every effort has been made to ensure the accuracy of information within this publication but the publishers cannot be held responsible for any errors or omissions. Views expressed are those of the author and do not necessarily represent those of the publishers or the football club. All rights reserved.

Photography © SNS Group.

ISBN 978-1-911287-06-3

CONTENTS

WELCOME

Welcome to the latest Official Hibernian Annual.

Season 2015/16 was a truly historic year for Hibernian Football Club. 21st May 2016 will be a date etched in the collective memory of Hibernian supporters for decades to come – the day the Club finally ended one of the longest-running, most talked about hoodoos in Scottish football, when the William Hill Scottish Cup was won.

When goal-scoring hero and Club captain David Gray lifted the famous old Cup above his head in celebration, the roar that greeted him was one of palpable joy and relief.

As Hampden reverberated to "Sunshine on Leith" it was impossible not to think back to 1902, to the last time Hibernian lifted the trophy, when the Hibernian President was Philip Farmer, great-grandfather of our own principal shareholder, Sir Tom Farmer.

The momentous moment last May was delivered to us by a dynamic young management team, led by Alan Stubbs, that was given its first opportunity here at Hibernian. While they left the Club shortly afterwards to return to England and the challenge of the Championship, Alan, John Doolan and Andy "Taff" Holden deserve all of our thanks. We wish them well in their future careers.

Our Cup exploits were tremendous last season. Not only did the Club lift the Scottish Cup, we were narrowly and undeservedly defeated by Ross County in the dying seconds of the final of the Scottish League Cup, presented by Utilita, earlier in the season after a great run to Hampden. That the team recovered so well from that huge disappointment speaks volumes for their characters.

Our major focus was on the league, and on gaining promotion. While we did not manage to achieve that, progress was again shown in the consistency and performances of the team, with the major exception being a difficult few weeks in March and April as the fixture pile-up caused by our cup exploits took an initial toll.

Now, we look ahead to the challenge again – and this season the challenge set is straightforward. We want to win the Ladbrokes Championship and return to the top flight automatically, as champions. In our new Head Coach Neil Lennon we have appointed a proven winner, an experienced and dynamic young manager who understands the pressure of having to win match after match after his successful tenure at Celtic.

As ever, your Board will do all that it can to back Neil in his efforts. We know that you, the supporters, will play your part to the full. Enjoy the Annual.

Rod Petrie, Chairman

LADBROKES CHAMPIONSHIP
SEASON REVIEW

SEPTEMBER

September saw the winning run continue, with a comfortable 3-0 home win against Alloa as Cummings, Liam Henderson and John McGinn all scored, and the following week saw a narrow 1-0 away win secured against Livingston courtesy of Henderson. The winning run ended with a 1-1 draw against St Mirren at Easter Road, with Martin Boyle netting for the Hibees.

AUGUST

The season kicked off with enormous media speculation and comment around the future of Scott Allan, with Rangers making public efforts to sign the player. Hibernian was steadfast in its refusal to sell to its biggest rivals for the league. On 8th August our first match was away to Dumbarton, and that was to end in a disappointing 2-1 defeat. A home match followed, with victory notched against Morton by 1-0, and the month ended with another league win, this time by 2-0 against Raith Rovers at Easter Road, with Jason Cummings and James Keatings both on the scoresheet.

NOVEMBER

Rangers were the visitors to Easter Road for the first match between the top fancied sides in the league at the start of November, and after a thrilling encounter the Hibs ran out 2-1 winners with Cummings and Paul Hanlon scoring for the boys in green. St Mirren were routed 4-1 in Paisley, with Keatings notching a hat-trick, and the month drew to a close with a home win against Livingston by 2-1, followed by a victory at Alloa by a single goal, scored by that man Cummings.

OCTOBER

What appeared a tricky trip to Dumfries to face Queen of the South was safely negotiated with a convincing 3-0 win, with Cummings again amongst the goals, and that was followed with a 4-2 win at Easter Road against Dumbarton with Cummings, Fontaine, Keatings and Malonga the scorers. Falkirk, who were to prove difficult opposition all season, were despatched 1-0 away, and this was followed by a 2-1 win in Kirkcaldy against Raith Rovers to end what had been a convincing month for Hibernian.

LADBROKES CHAMPIONSHIP
SEASON REVIEW

JANUARY

The New Year saw Raith Rovers come to Easter Road on 2nd January, with Hibernian winners by a solitary Jason Cummings goal. Falkirk away was next on league business, with a 1-1 draw again showing the tough and competitive nature of matches against this opponent. The league campaign for the month ended with a home match against St Mirren, which Hibernian won 3-1 with Henderson and McGinn amongst the scorers.

DECEMBER

December kicked off with a hard-fought 1-1 draw at Easter Road against Falkirk, with Hibernian reduced to ten men following John McGinn's red card. Queen of the South were next to visit, with Hibernian running out 1-0 winners. 28th December saw Hibs travel west to face Rangers again, at a packed and hostile Ibrox, with the Glasgow team running out 4-2 winners and Cummings again on the scoresheet against the Ibrox side.

FEBRUARY

Greenock was the destination at the start of February, with Hibernian defeating Morton 1-0 under the floodlights through an Anthony Stokes goal. Livingston was next up, again away from home, and a nil each draw was fought out in poor conditions. February ended with three matches in little over a week, as the fixture congestion caused by the Club's successful cup runs caught up. Alloa were defeated 3-0 at Easter Road, with Cummings scoring two of them, and then Morton inflicted a shock 3-0 defeat on Hibernian at Easter Road. This was to set off a run of poor results that had a huge impact on league hopes. The month ended with another away defeat to Dumbarton, by 3-2, despite a thrilling Hibernian comeback in the second half from 3-0 down.

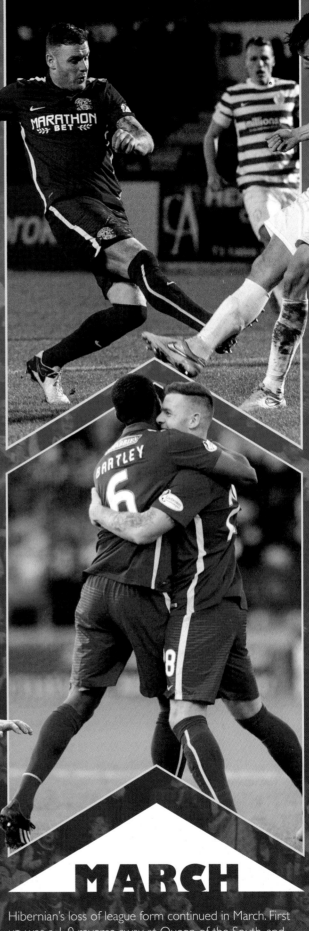

MARCH

Hibernian's loss of league form continued in March. First up was a 1-0 reverse away at Queen of the South, and this was followed by defeat in Kirkcaldy to Raith Rovers by 2-1, with Stokes again scoring for Hibs. The month also saw Hibernian's great run in the League Cup end in disappointment with a 1-0 defeat to Ross County, but more of that elsewhere.

LADBROKES CHAMPIONSHIP
SEASON REVIEW

APRIL

April saw the club's fixture congestion reach a peak, with seven league matches scheduled for the month. A 2-2 draw in Paisley against St Mirren was followed by a 2-1 win at home against Livingston, with Stokes in the goals again. A 1-0 defeat away to Alloa was followed by a 2-2 draw at Easter Road against rivals Falkirk, disappointing, as Hibs were 2-0 up with just minutes to play and suffered a rare late collapse. Rangers were defeated 3-2 at Easter Road in a thrilling match, with Cummings and Gunnarson scoring, and this was followed by a nil each draw away to Morton. The month ended with a thumping 4-0 defeat of Dumbarton at Easter Road, with Keatings notching two.

MAY

The league campaign entered its final month with a 2-0 defeat of Queen of the South at Easter Road meaning Hibernian finished third, behind champions Rangers and also behind Falkirk on goal difference. That finish meant the Easter Road side were consigned to play a tough schedule of play-off matches, with Raith Rovers, who had finished fourth, first up.

A 1-0 defeat away to Raith Rovers saw the possibility that Hibernian might exit the play-offs at the first hurdle, but a strong early showing in the return at Easter Road saw the team score two without reply, via McGinn and Darren McGregor, to set up a play-off semi-final show-down with Falkirk.

The first tie at Easter Road ended in a 2-2 draw which was harsh on Hibernian who had led comfortably until a very late rally by Falkirk, allied with some nervous defending, saw the visitors level. While a strong Hibernian claim for a penalty was also denied earlier in the match, the opportunity still existed to win at Falkirk, and Hibernian were on course with just twelve minutes to go, leading through a Keatings double, when Falkirk scored an equaliser. The winner, agonisingly, came with just seconds remaining as Falkirk again showed their fighting spirit to win through and end Hibernian's hopes of a return to Scotland's top flight for another season.

But the William Hill Scottish Cup Final was still in the Club's sights…

NEIL LENNON

The appointment of Neil Lennon as Head Coach at Hibernian was regarded as a coup as the Club brought in the experienced and highly-regarded former Celtic boss to spearhead the push for promotion.

The tough, no-nonsense Northern Irishman was seen as the perfect man to come in following the departure of Alan Stubbs to the English Championship.

He arrived with a stark warning – to tackle the inconsistency which had cost the Club in its previous efforts to gain promotion. "I don't want the players getting pats on the back for beating Raith Rovers or drawing away at Dumbarton. I'll give them a pat on the back if they get promotion. Inconsistency won't be tolerated. It's not acceptable at a Club of this standing."

He was quick to add a note of praise however. "I think the lads showed great character in coming from behind against Rangers to win the Scottish Cup and get that particular monkey off the club's back. It was a great achievement by the players but I don't want them dining out on that. When their careers are over they can do that but it's important that we get out of this division now."

He has promised to respect the Club's traditions, in particular the desire of the fans to see exciting, attacking football – a demand he was well used to during his successful spell at Celtic when he took the Club into the last sixteen of the Champions' League.

He said: "There's nothing wrong with good football if you get goals but, at times, you need to mix it up a little bit and you need to be physical. It's not easy playing in Scotland.

"At Celtic, everyone wanted to beat you because you were the best team. Everyone raised their game that little bit extra and you have to have a mentality to get used to that."

His philosophy reflects his own playing career, as a talented but often under-rated midfielder who anchored some notable teams, including Manchester City, Leicester City and – of course – a strong Celtic side under Martin O'Neill.

During his career, he made around 600 appearances at senior level, including 40 caps for Northern Ireland. His medal haul makes impressive reading – 5 SPL titles, 4 Scottish Cup winner medals, 2 Scottish League Cup medals, 2 English League Cup medals won with Leicester, and a runners-up medal in the UEFA Cup.

As a manager, he has added 3 SPL titles and 2 Scottish Cups.

He became Celtic manager in 2010, guiding them to numerous titles and that exciting Champions League journey, which also saw Celtic defeat Barcelona. He held the position for four years, before leaving and joining Bolton in October 2014.

However, the Lancashire club's financial woes made the task virtually impossible. He managed to keep the Club in the Championship in his first season, but, with little budget and the club struggling, left the following year.

He said: "You learn from it. I think the issues I faced at Bolton are well known, but you learn from it and it makes you a stronger person and a better manager."

WILLIAM HILL
SCOTTISH
CUP QUIZ

1 Prior to May 2016, in which year did Hibernian last win the Scottish Cup?

2 Which player captained Hibernian to League Cup success in 2007?

3 Which current Hibernian star was named Man of the Match that day?

4 Name the team who provided the opposition in 2007?

5 Name the Moroccan striker who scored twice in the 2007 win?

6 Which Hibernian legend managed Aberdeen to a Scottish Cup win?

7 Name the goalscoring legend who scored in Hibernian's 2-0 league cup win over Dunfermline in season 1991/92.

8 Who skippered Hibs to victory with a Man of the Match performance in the 1972 League Cup final?

9 Which team did Hibernian defeat to lift the trophy that day?

10 Who was manager of Hibernian when they won the Scottish Cup in 1902?

Answers on page 58.

NEW SIGNING

Andrew Shinnie

Andrew Shinnie was one of Head Coach Neil Lennon's key recruitments when the 27-year-old midfielder arrived on loan from Birmingham City in the summer.

The 27-year-old is no stranger to Scottish football, having begun his career at Rangers – with loan spells in Dundee - before enjoying a successful spell in the Highlands with Inverness Caledonian Thistle.

A technical and gifted player, he is an attacking talent and one who likes to get on the scoresheet. While at Inverness, his performances were of such quality that he earned a full international cap – to date his only international appearance – making a substitute appearance against Luxembourg.

Neil Lennon said: "Andrew is a quality player, strong and very good technically, and provides a goal threat. I liked him when he was at Inverness. He is at a good stage in his career, he has experience but he is physically in his prime, so we are delighted that he has chosen to come to Hibernian to help us in our league campaign."

The player – who appeared for Birmingham against Hibernian in a pre-season friendly at Easter Road - said: "I am delighted to be part of a strong Hibernian squad that aims to return the Club to the top flight of Scottish football. It is a big Club, with big ambition and a top manager."

HIBS LAST SCOTTISH CUP WIN

By Tom Wright, Club Historian

The incredible scenes that met the 2016 Scottish Cup winners as they made their way by open top bus through Edinburgh will linger long in the minds of all those who were present. It is estimated that well over 150,000 crowded the streets to celebrate, the east side of the city completely bathed in a sea of green and white.

Similar jubilation gripped the city in 1902 when huge crowds – though not quite so massive - turned out to welcome the Scottish Cup back to Easter Road.

At the turn of the last century, Hibs were one of the most attractive sides in the country. During the 1901-02 season, however, league results had been less than satisfactory, only six games won from a total of eighteen with four drawn, but in the Scottish Cup it was a drastically different story. The road to Hampden began with a 2-0 victory over Clyde at Easter Road, followed by a convincing 5-1 away defeat of Port Glasgow Athletic. An even more emphatic 7-1 victory against Queens Park in the third round set up a semi-final meeting with Rangers at Ibrox.

League Champions Rangers were favourites on the day but over 30,000, including many who had travelled through from the capital by special train, saw the Edinburgh side rise to the occasion to record a notable 2-0 victory to set up a meeting with Celtic in the final.

With work still taking place at the new national stadium at Hampden, the cup final was to have taken place at Ibrox on Saturday 12 April 1902. Unfortunately, during the Scotland versus England international at the same ground seven days before, 25 people were killed and well over 500 injured when part of the wooden terracing behind one of the goals collapsed, and the final was temporarily postponed. It was later decided that even although it was the home ground of one of the finalists, the game would now go ahead at Parkhead a few weeks later on Saturday 26th April 1902.

Celtic had been installed as red hot favourites, not only because of the advantage of playing on home turf, but also because they had won two of the previous three finals.

HIBERNIAN FOOTBALL CLUB.
WINNERS OF SCOTTISH CUP, GLASGOW CHARITY CUP, ROSEBERY CUP, and M'CRAE CUP, 1902,

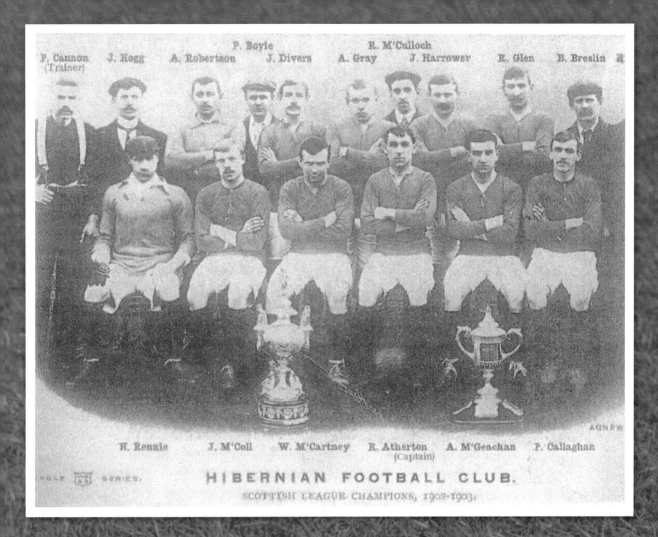

P. Cannon (Trainer)   J. Hogg   A. Robertson   P. Boyle   J. Divers   R. M'Culloch   A. Gray   J. Harrower   R. Glen   B. Breslin

H. Rennie   J. M'Coll   W. M'Cartney   R. Atherton (Captain)   A. M'Geachan   P. Callaghan

HIBERNIAN FOOTBALL CLUB.

SCOTTISH LEAGUE CHAMPIONS, 1902-1903.

AGNEW

At the kick off it was obvious that the swirling wind blowing from goalmouth to goalmouth would make good football difficult for both sides and spoil the game as a spectacle for the 16,000 fans packed into the ground. Playing with the wind at their back, predictably Celtic were the more direct and dangerous in the first half although rarely troubling the Easter Road defence.

In the second half Hibs began to use the blustery conditions to their advantage and looked the most likely side to score although there was an almighty scare for the Easter Road side when Celtic hit the post before the ball was eventually cleared to safety. Continuing to assert themselves in the difficult conditions, midway through the second half Welsh cap Bobby Atherton thought he had opened the scoring only for the goal to be disallowed for offside. A goal was not long in coming however. With just 15 minutes remaining Callaghan took a corner on Hibs right and, according to legend, Atherton's shout for a Celtic defender to 'leave it' allowed the tricky McGeachan to cheekily back heel the ball into the net. Disputed or not, it was the goal that would decide the Cup.

At the final whistle the thousands of Hibs fans who had made their way from the Capital were in ecstatic mood, the Easter Road players leaving the field to exalted acclaim.

At a short ceremony in the Alexander Hotel in Glasgow, the Hibernian President Phillip Farmer was presented with the trophy, before the victorious Hibs side made their way to Queen Street Station for the trip to Edinburgh. Arrangements had earlier been made for the Hibs party to disembark at Haymarket where they were met by a huge crowd, the rousing strains of a brass band, and a

four in hand waiting to transport the players and officials on their victory parade along Princes Street, down Leith Street and along London Road to the ground. Everywhere the route was crammed with jubilant supporters, all aware of what a momentous occasion it was for the city, the traffic brought to a grinding halt at the bottleneck of North Bridge and Waterloo Place by a mass of excited bodies. Later, the celebrations would continue long into the night.

It had been an incredible journey since 1893. Memories of the dark days of only a few years before when the club had stared extinction in the face, had now been banished forever, and it was to be only the start. The Scottish Cup success had brought an invitation to take part in the Glasgow Charity Cup a few weeks later. After yet another cup victory over Rangers, Hibs would emphasise their superiority over the Glasgow greens by defeating Celtic 6-2 in the Hampden (Cathkin) final.

It would not end there. At the end of the following season Hibernian Football Club would be crowned Scottish League Champions for the first time in the club's history, a 2-0 victory against Partick Thistle at Meadowside just a few days before Christmas was enough to secure the championship with two games still to play. Of the Hibs players that lined up that momentous afternoon, seven had taken part in the previous season's cup final.

The Hibs team that won the Scottish Cup that afternoon was:

Rennie, Gray and Glen, Breslin, Harrower and Robertson, McColl, McGeachan, Divers, Callaghan and Atherton.

GLORY, GLORY
TO THE HIBEES

While more than 20,000 Hibees sang "Sunshine on Leith" to greet a history-making day at Hampden on 21st May 2016, the road to glory started much earlier in the season.

Shortly after New Year, on 9th January, Hibs travelled to Kirkcaldy to take on high-flying Raith Rovers in a tough away fourth-round cup tie. The big Hibernian travelling support were in confident mood, and that proved justified as the team produced a professional performance to win 2-0.

It would be all about the name that came out of the hat, and in the 5th round Hibernian were handed one of the toughest of draws – but one that whet the appetite and set the Capital talking – when we were drawn away to arch-rivals Hearts at Tynecastle.

The match appeared to be running away from the men in green and white, with Hearts taking a 2-0 lead and looking as if they would see out the match, despite Hibernian playing much of the attacking football. Then Jason Cummings struck with a looping header well into the second half. That sparked a stirring fightback, capped very late in the match when Paul Hanlon slid home an equaliser to send the away fans home delirious.

The replay, at Easter Road, was still a tough challenge, with the men in maroon enjoying a strong return to Scotland's top flight and in an excellent run of form. But an early strike from Cummings settled the nerves, and while Hearts huffed and puffed they rarely threatened to break Hibs down and it was the Easter Road side who went into the quarter finals.

The task was to become no easier. Cup holders Inverness awaited Hibernian. Even with home advantage, Hibernian knew they would need to be on top form to progress. The tie finished 1-1, with Keatings the scorer, and it was off to the Highland Capital for the replay. Anthony Stokes was to prove the talisman, with two goals vital in a hard fought 2-1 win that saw Hibernian into the semis.

Dundee United were struggling for league form, but had enjoyed a good cup run. With neutral Hampden the venue, the two sides were evenly matched in a nervy encounter which eventually went into extra time after finishing goalless – but only after Jason Cummings had missed a penalty in spectacular fashion. Penalties beckoned, and debut goalkeeper Conrad Logan was to prove the hero with his saves, but let's not forget the expertly despatched penalties which ensured the win also.

So it was on to the final, to play old rivals Rangers in the first ever Scottish Cup final played by two sides from outwith the top flight of Scottish football.

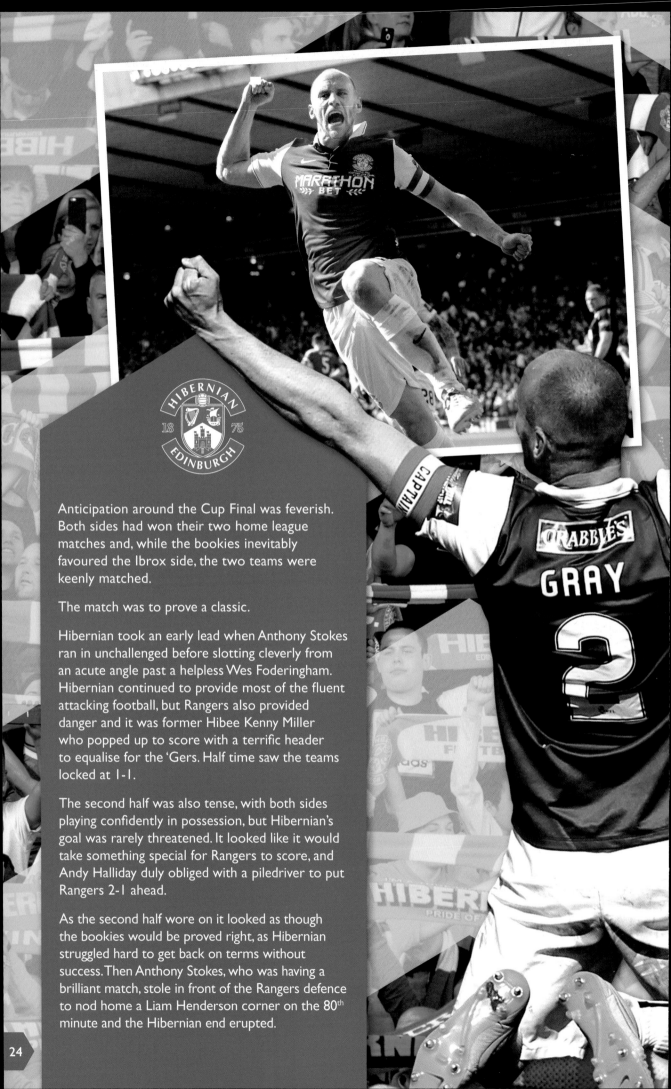

Anticipation around the Cup Final was feverish. Both sides had won their two home league matches and, while the bookies inevitably favoured the Ibrox side, the two teams were keenly matched.

The match was to prove a classic.

Hibernian took an early lead when Anthony Stokes ran in unchallenged before slotting cleverly from an acute angle past a helpless Wes Foderingham. Hibernian continued to provide most of the fluent attacking football, but Rangers also provided danger and it was former Hibee Kenny Miller who popped up to score with a terrific header to equalise for the 'Gers. Half time saw the teams locked at 1-1.

The second half was also tense, with both sides playing confidently in possession, but Hibernian's goal was rarely threatened. It looked like it would take something special for Rangers to score, and Andy Halliday duly obliged with a piledriver to put Rangers 2-1 ahead.

As the second half wore on it looked as though the bookies would be proved right, as Hibernian struggled hard to get back on terms without success. Then Anthony Stokes, who was having a brilliant match, stole in front of the Rangers defence to nod home a Liam Henderson corner on the 80th minute and the Hibernian end erupted.

25

That saw Hibernian take command, and push for a winner, but the match appeared to be heading for extra time when, deep into stoppage time, another Liam Henderson corner was met by skipper David Gray who superbly headed into the net for a late winner that broke Rangers' hearts.

The Hibernian fans joy was complete. To end a 114 year hoodoo, to beat one of Scotland's biggest clubs to do it, and to win in the dying seconds all contributed to emotional scenes as the Club finally lifted the trophy that had eluded them for so long.

At last the Club could put into action plans for a Victory Parade to show supporters the Cup – and what a Sunday that proved to be.

Approximately 150,000 took to the streets to enjoy the day and, in fine sunshine, the Cup was paraded from a civic reception at the Regional Chambers, down the Royal Mile, down North Bridge and across the east end of Princes Street, and on down Leith Street. Huge crowds crammed the pavements, with thousands following on behind the bus as it slowly made its way through the Capital.

The sight that greeted the team on Leith Walk was truly extraordinary, with an estimated 70,000 plus out on the famous old thoroughfare to welcome the Cup.

Then it was on down to Leith Links, to a party, with another 25,000 cramming the area to celebrate with songs and applause, led by skipper Gray. A weekend to remember forever for all Hibees fortunate to have witnessed it.

EUROPEAN PIONEERS RETURN TO BIG STAGE

As if winning the William Hill Scottish Cup after a wait of 114 years wasn't enough reason for joy amongst Hibernian fans, there was one keenly anticipated "bonus".

Lifting the trophy meant a return to European football for the team who were the first British club to enter European competition back in the 1950s.

The UEFA Europa League draw saw Hibernian given the toughest draw faced by any of the qualifying Scottish sides, a tie against crack Danish side Brondby. The Copenhagen club are experienced and wily European campaigners with a big playing budget.

The first match took place at Easter Road under the floodlights on the 14th of July, and the match got off to the worst possible start for young Finnish goalie Otso Virtanen when he spilled an apparently harmless shot at the feet of a Brondby striker, who promptly tapped home with just a few seconds on the clock.

Both teams locked horns in an enthralling contest for the remainder of the 90 minutes, which was not without controversy as Hibernian were denied a strong penalty claim and had a goal wrongly chalked off for offside by the Spanish match officials.

A 0-1 home reverse meant the return to Copenhagen was an uphill task, but Head Coach Neil Lennon had seen much to encourage him.

Almost 1,000 Hibernian fans made the short journey to Copenhagen a week later – many by circuitous routes – to cheer on the team, and the supporters made the most of their trip by enjoying the Scandinavian heatwave to the full, relaxing in the bars and cafes, and congregating around The Dubliner pub to sing their songs and enjoy friendly banter with the locals.

At Brondby Stadium a clever game-plan saw Hibernian stifle the physical Danish side before grabbing a dramatic goal after around an hour through skipper David Gray.

The team then held on heroically, while displaying real menace on the counter, and even extra time failed to separate the two teams. The tie was destined for a penalty shoot-out. Brondby's skipper was first up and found the net, despite a valiant effort from rookie debutant goalkeeper Ross Laidlaw. John McGinn was up for Hibernian, and his effort was saved leaving the young midfield powerhouse disconsolate. Brondby showed great composure and despite Hibernian scoring the rest of their penalties taken, it was the Danes who scraped through by the narrowest of margins.

Hibernian's fans, who had been terrific in backing the team throughout the trip, continued to give their support, reserving a special rendition of "We've got McGinn, Super John McGinn" for the disappointed youngster.

PLAYER PROFILES

David Gray

David Gray – Hibernian captain and cup-winning legend. David was Alan Stubbs's first signing when he joined the Club in July 2014, and his no-nonsense defending and attacking forays have established him as a firm favourite with supporters.

His professionalism and leadership have also seen him lead the team as captain, and his qualities were never more evident than during the Scottish Cup Final against Rangers in May 2016, when a brilliant performance was capped with his late, winning, headed goal.

The right-back brings all of his experience and ability to bear in every game, having enjoyed spells at Manchester United and Preston North End amongst others.

Otso Virtanen

Otso Virtanen joined Hibernian on a three-and-a-half year deal in the summer of 2016.

The big Finn, who stands 6ft 5ins, has kept goal for his country at under-21 level.

He joined Hibs from Finnish top flight side IFK Mariehamn, and has played around 100 league games at that level.

Lewis Stevenson

Lewis is that rare breed, a one-club professional who is Hibernian's longest-serving player and is in his testimonial year. But it's more than simple longevity that has made the left-back such an enduringly popular figure with supporters.

His commitment to the Hibernian cause can never be questioned, his attitude earning plaudits from every manager he has worked with, and he is a real team player. Lewis can also claim a place as a club legend.

His man-of-the-match performance in the League Cup win of 2007, plus his role in May 2016 for the Scottish Cup win, means he is the only Hibernian player ever to have won both the Scottish Cup and the League Cup.

Paul Hanlon

Edinburgh-born Paul Hanlon, like his defensive mate Lewis Stevenson, is a dyed-in-the-wool Hibee.

The big centre back is another product of the Hibernian Academy, and has been in the Hibernian first team for several seasons, notching up more than 250 appearances. Cultured, mobile, and a goal threat at set plays, Paul's is one of the first names on the team sheet whether as part of a back four or in a three.

He has been capped at under-19 level for Scotland, and is a former under-21 international skipper.

Darren McGregor

When Darren McGregor signed for Hibernian in August 2015 from Rangers, he was joining the Club he had supported since boyhood.

The proud Leither, the Ibrox side's Player of the Year in 2014/15, was surprisingly released by the Glasgow club and Hibernian moved swiftly to clinch his signature – and what a good signing the big defender proved to be.

Now firmly established in the team, Darren's solid displays and occasional goals have proven invaluable – as have his experience and his mobility.

Liam Fontaine

Experienced defender Liam Fontaine enjoyed a wealth of experience in the Championship in England before signing for Hibernian in August 2014.

The big centre-back spent eight years at Bristol City, and also enjoyed a spell at Fulham.

When he arrived at Easter Road, it wasn't his first foray north of the border. Liam also spent some time at Kilmarnock on loan.

Jordon Forster

Jordon Forster is another Edinburgh-born player, who joined Hibernian at the age of 16 from Celtic's Youth Academy.

He made his debut, memorably, in a derby win against Hearts at Tynecastle, giving an assured performance in the middle of the Hibernian defence during the 2012/13 season.

Jordon spent last season on loan at Plymouth. He can play at centre half or at right back.

Marvin Bartley

Marvin Bartley is another signing who joined Hibernian after enjoying significant experience in England's Championship.

Marvin, who plays the anchor role in midfield, has had spells with a number of good clubs down south, including Bournemouth, Burnley and Leyton Orient.

His tough tackling, simple-but-effective style has made him a firm favourite with both fans and coaches, and he played a key role in last season's successes.

John McGinn

Many pundits were surprised when Hibernian managed to clinch the signature of midfielder John McGinn in the summer of 2015 – an undisclosed fee paid to St Mirren beating off competition from a number of Scottish clubs and interest from the United States.

Given the Club's place outside the top flight of Scottish football, some expressed doubts about his decision to come to Easter Road.

But the talented player has never looked back, turning in a series of man-of-the-match performances and making his full international debut, winning the Scottish Cup and earning his own song from supporters happy to know that "We've got McGinn, Super John McGinn."

Fraser Fyvie

Fraser Fyvie has established himself as a key player in the middle of the park for Hibernian, after originally joining on a short term loan.

A former Scotland under-21 international, Fraser joined Hibs after spending two-and-a-half years with Wigan, and was on the bench when that club secured an FA Cup win.

He went one better in May 2016, when Fraser played in the Scottish Cup win against Rangers to add a Scottish Cup medal to his collection.

Dylan McGeouch

A successful loan spell at Easter Road in season 2014/15 saw attacking midfielder Dylan McGeouch sign permanently last summer from Celtic for an undisclosed fee.

An energetic and dynamic player, McGeouch was an important and fresh player at the end of the season after recovering from a lengthy injury.

His all-action performances mean Dylan is an important part of the club's midfield mix. Dylan is another who has played for Scotland at under-21 level.

Brian Graham

Striker Brian Graham joined Hibernian in the summer on a two-year deal.

The 6ft 2in attacker joined from top flight side Ross County, after making a flying start to the season banging in the goals for the Dingwall club.

He was recruited by Head Coach Neil Lennon to provide greater competition for the striking positions, offer a different option, and reinforce the Club's drive for promotion. Brian has played for a number of Scottish sides, including Dundee United, St Johnstone and Raith Rovers.

Grant Holt

Grant Holt joined Hibernian in the summer, Neil Lennon's first new signing as Head Coach.

The big striker has played at just about every level south of the border, and during a successful spell at Norwich City in the Premier League was tipped for a call-up to the England national side.

A powerful, experienced, skilful player he will help bring out the best in his younger fellow strikers at Easter Road.

Jason Cummings

Jason Cummings extended his contract with Hibernian in the summer – bringing cheers from Hibernian fans who have enjoyed watching the progress of this exciting young goalscorer.

Jason's goal tally last season marked him out as the club's top marksman, and his vital goals helped Hibernian to cup glory as well as securing important league points.

Left sided, Jason joined Hibernian in the summer of 2013 from Hutchison Vale. He was famously working as a gardener at that time, having left the youth system at Hearts.

Martin Boyle

Martin Boyle joined the club on loan from Dundee during the 2014/15 season, after helping the Tayside club gain promotion to the top flight, making his debut in an Edinburgh derby.

He signed a full contract with Hibernian the following season, and quickly secured his place in the first team squad.

Pacy and direct, Martin can play wide or through the middle.

39

James Keatings

Striker James Keatings played a big role in Hibernian's season last year, and will be building on that during this season.

Originally with Celtic, James has also had spells at Hamilton Academicals and at Hearts, helping both clubs win promotion to the Scottish Premiership.

He will be hoping to make it a unique hat-trick this season.

Ross Laidlaw

Hibs signed former Raith Rovers goalkeeper Ross Laidlaw on a one-year contract during the summer, after the 23-year-old had impressed in training at East Mains.

The big goalie, who had been at Raith Rovers for five years, was pitched into Europa League action in Copenhagen against Danish cracks Brondby, where he played his part with a terrific display to help the Club keep a clean sheet and win a difficult away tie 1-0, although the team was to undeservedly go out on penalties.

GAMECHANGER

A big part of Hibernian's work in our community comes from its GameChanger project – a partnership involving the Club, NHS Lothian, and the Hibernian Community Foundation.

This project has been set up to harness the Club's assets – such as the stadium and the training ground – to promote positive health and social outcomes by using the power and reach of football.

As part of GameChanger, kids from the local community got the opportunity to hit the

streets of Leith a week after our Cup Final win to interview fans and the general public about their thoughts on Hibs historic Scottish Cup win. The children and young adults involved had never before had the chance to use cameras and microphones and it was fun-filled day for all involved.

Iain Shaw from Media Education who partnered with GameChanger to make the event happen said, "All the young

people did brilliantly. They had less than an hour to learn how the cameras work and to practice their interviews before they were out on to the streets of Leith and talking to everyone they met. I was very impressed with how quickly they picked up the camera and interview skills and just gave it a go. You could really tell that they're all devoted fans through the quality of the questions they asked. I think they would be an asset for Hibs TV."

GAMECHANGER

SPOT THE BALL

Can you guess which is the real ball?

Answer on page 58.

SIGN UP FOR HIBS KIDS

Hibs Kids' memberships are available for 0-11 year olds, with the following included in their £15 membership:

- A ticket to four Hibs Kids' matches in a season (two before Christmas, and two after).
- Hibs Kid membership card which can be used to gain access to Easter Road on matchdays*.
- A birthday card delivered to your registered address.
- Hibernian FC wallchart.
- Hibernian FC sticker.
- The opportunity to be a mascot at a Hibernian home league match.

Season ticket holders are automatically Hibs Kids' members, and will receive their wallchart and sticker in the coming weeks, as well as a birthday card on their special day. To join Hibs Kids simply purchase a membership online through the Hibernian e-Ticketing site or visit the Hibernian Ticket Office.

Designated Hibs Kids' matches for this season:
- Hibernian v Ayr United, 17 September 2016
- Hibernian v Dumbarton, 10 December 2016
- Hibernian v Greenock Morton, 4 March 2017
- Hibernian v Queen of the South, 15 April 2017

*Please note cards are activated by purchase of match tickets.

Hibs Kids must be accompanied by an adult at matches.

LEWIS STEVENSON

Tony Mowbray, during his stint as Manager at Hibernian, liked to use a range of inspirational quotes to motivate his team. One of his favourites was from General George S Patton: "It's not the size of the dog in the fight that counts, but the size of the fight in the dog."

That quote fits Lewis Stevenson better than just about any other player. Hibernian's longest-serving player, Fifer Lewis is enjoying his testimonial season this year, a one Club man in an age of journeymen.

But it isn't just his loyalty for the Club he loves that inspires such affection for the 5ft 7in left back amongst the Hibernian support. His never-say-die spirit, his determination and courage, and his unwillingness to hide when times are tough have all seen him forge a genuine bond with fans.

And clearly, several managers have agreed with the supporters' assessment. Lewis has been a regular starter under all of our recent managers, with all of them praising him as the "model professional."

Lewis has been through the highs and lows as a Hibernian player. But nothing has surpassed the joy he experienced on 21st May. "We can imagine the pain we have put Hibs fans through – I've felt it myself. But the euphoria we have today takes away every low we've had. I thought I was destined for failure to be honest. Thank God I wasn't."

He certainly wasn't. In fact, Lewis has a unique place in the history of Hibernian as the first man ever to win League and Scottish Cup medals as a Hibs player – a special double. Lewis played his part in the run to William Hill Scottish Cup glory, and was Man of the Match in the famous 2007 League Cup win against Kilmarnock.

Lewis made his competitive debut in 2005 in a cup tie against Ayr United, but he had to wait for the first match of the 2006/07 league campaign to make his league debut. Since then, he has amassed 320 appearances for Hibernian.

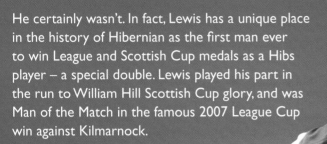

Typically, Lewis is modest about his place in the Club's pantheon: "I'm not daft, there's been loads of players who are miles better than me who have been at Hibs. They've tried to get the Scottish Cup but haven't quite managed to do it. But for myself and the players here it's impossible to describe this feeling."

Here's to many more games…

JOHN McGINN

As the open-top bus trundled slowly past tens of thousands of delirious Hibernian supporters, parading the Scottish Cup, one song cropped up at every stage…

"We've got McGinn, Super John McGinn," echoed throughout the Capital as the supporters paid homage to their heroes.

The man in whose honour they sang has already placed himself firmly at the heart of the affections of Hibernian supporters for his uncompromising style, his inventive play, and his strong tackling.

John, who turned 22 in October this year, came to the Club from St Mirren in the summer of 2015 after the two clubs agreed compensation. He had already played for Scotland at under 19 and under 21 levels, and Hibs saw off competition from home and abroad for his services.

A number of stellar performances, including a strong showing in the William Hill Scottish Cup final, has seen the young midfield player's star shine even brighter, and his call up to the full national squad saw him make his full debut and produce a Man of the Match display. He was named as the SPFL Championship Player of the Year.

John is now the proud owner of a League Cup winners' medal won in 2013 with the Buddies, and his prized Scottish Cup medal, but he is keen for more. And he sees his future at Hibs.

"It is a privilege to be at a club the size of Hibs. I had opportunities to go to Premiership clubs but I just felt I would be involved in high-pressure games, and I feel that has been justified.

"I am just determined to get Hibs back playing top-flight football. It is important for someone of my age to be playing at the highest level I can and that is the same for the other boys in the dressing room."

Despite the Club's failure to win promotion last season, John was reassured when national team boss Gordon Strachan reassured him that he would still be in his plans: "To put on the blue jersey was an incredible feeling and it has made me hungry to get more caps.

"Hopefully, if I keep playing well for my club, then that could happen.

"I feel as if I made a good impression so I want to keep doing that and get better and better."

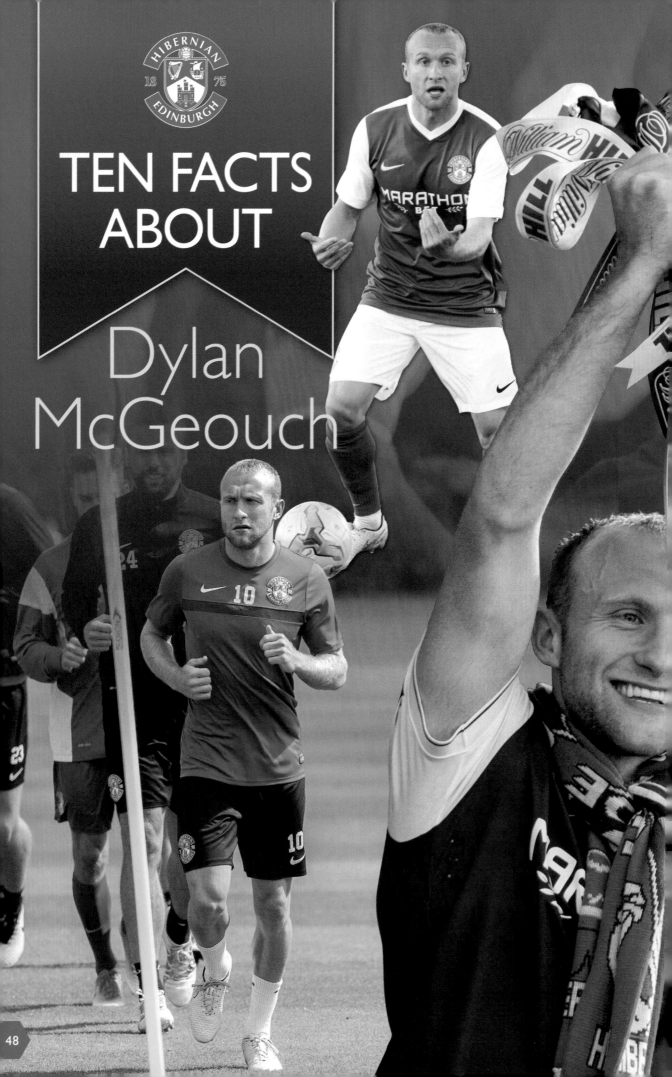

TEN FACTS ABOUT

Dylan McGeouch

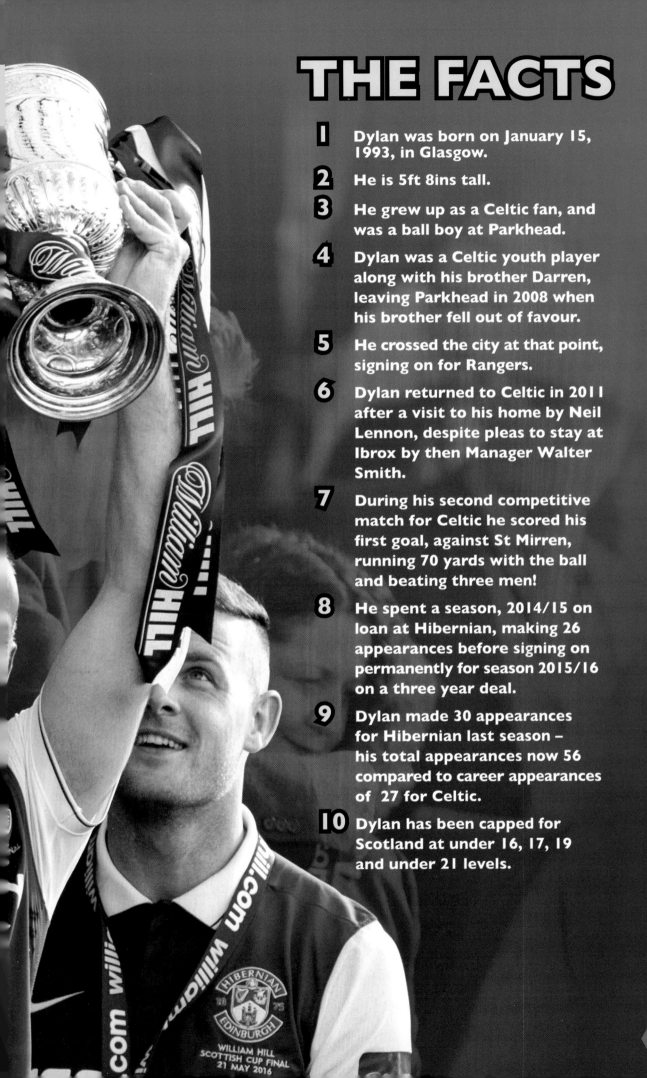

THE FACTS

1. Dylan was born on January 15, 1993, in Glasgow.

2. He is 5ft 8ins tall.

3. He grew up as a Celtic fan, and was a ball boy at Parkhead.

4. Dylan was a Celtic youth player along with his brother Darren, leaving Parkhead in 2008 when his brother fell out of favour.

5. He crossed the city at that point, signing on for Rangers.

6. Dylan returned to Celtic in 2011 after a visit to his home by Neil Lennon, despite pleas to stay at Ibrox by then Manager Walter Smith.

7. During his second competitive match for Celtic he scored his first goal, against St Mirren, running 70 yards with the ball and beating three men!

8. He spent a season, 2014/15 on loan at Hibernian, making 26 appearances before signing on permanently for season 2015/16 on a three year deal.

9. Dylan made 30 appearances for Hibernian last season – his total appearances now 56 compared to career appearances of 27 for Celtic.

10. Dylan has been capped for Scotland at under 16, 17, 19 and under 21 levels.

Ones to Watch

This season, a number of young stars at Hibernian will be hoping to make the big step up to become regular members of Neil Lennon's first team squad.

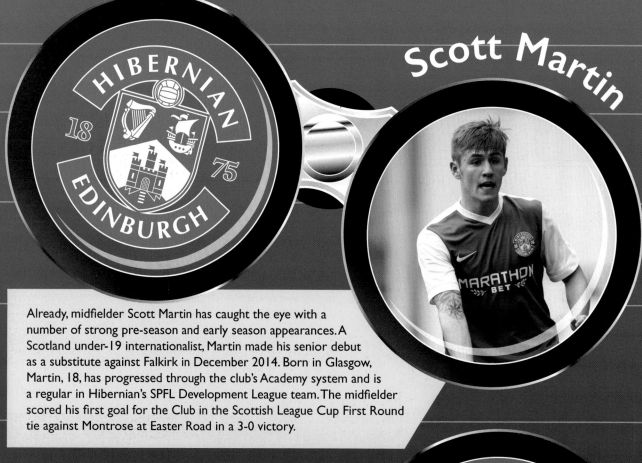

Scott Martin

Already, midfielder Scott Martin has caught the eye with a number of strong pre-season and early season appearances. A Scotland under-19 internationalist, Martin made his senior debut as a substitute against Falkirk in December 2014. Born in Glasgow, Martin, 18, has progressed through the club's Academy system and is a regular in Hibernian's SPFL Development League team. The midfielder scored his first goal for the Club in the Scottish League Cup First Round tie against Montrose at Easter Road in a 3-0 victory.

Callum Crane

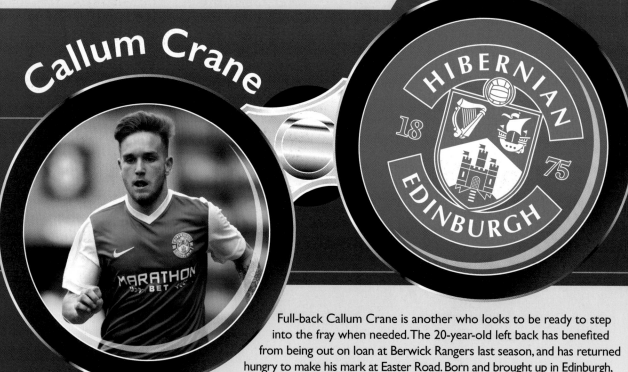

Full-back Callum Crane is another who looks to be ready to step into the fray when needed. The 20-year-old left back has benefited from being out on loan at Berwick Rangers last season, and has returned hungry to make his mark at Easter Road. Born and brought up in Edinburgh, Callum has come right through the Academy system after signing from AC Oxgangs. He has performed well when given the opportunity in matches this season, impressing teammates and coaches alike.

Oli Shaw

Another whose progress is being keenly monitored is young striker Oli Shaw. The 18-year-old – another Edinburgh-born member of the Hibernian Academy – has been a regular feature in the club's Development Squad, scoring regularly and catching the eye. Earlier this year he scored four in a 5-3 win over Partick Thistle.

Aaron Dunsmore

Aaron will be hoping that the six month loan spell he is currently enjoying with near neighbours Edinburgh City in league 2 will help kick on his career at Hibernian. The 20-year-old defender appeared in three pre-season matches for the Hibees in the summer, and has been sent out on loan by Head Coach Neil Lennon to get regular football to accelerate his development.

The right-back is a lifelong supporter of the Club, and is determined to make the breakthrough and play a part in the first-team squad at some point this season, having enjoyed his taste of action. He said: "I'm from Musselburgh, which is just down the road from Easter Road and I used to come and watch Hibs play regularly. "Overall it was a great experience and its one that I would love to taste again sometime soon."

NEW SIGNING

Ofir Marciano

Goalkeeper Ofir Marciano arrived in August from FC Ashdod of Israel on a season-long loan deal.

Ofir is an Israeli internationalist with several competitive caps to his name and has previously played in the top two tiers of domestic football in Israel and with Royal Excel Mouscron in the Belgian Pro League.

The 26-year-old goalie said on joining that he was excited at the prospect of playing in Scotland to help Hibernian achieve the club's main ambition of promotion back to the top flight of football in Scotland.

An impressive 6ft 4ins tall, Ofir spoke with international teammate Nir Bitton of Celtic before making the move.

He said: "I am excited to be in Scotland, playing at a big club with real ambition. I know how passionate supporters are here about their football."

HIBERNIAN
HERO

Some players are loved by fans because of their outstanding footballing skills, others for their homegrown love of a club.

But – while no mean player – former Hibernian hero Dirk Lehmann's cult status with supporters owes more to his outgoing personality and his unique sense of style.

The striker who enjoyed his stay in Edinburgh under Alex McLeish from 1999 – 2001 was distinctive wherever he played, with his well-groomed moustache and his pierced, studded ears.

His earlobes, in particular, drew attention. Rather than seek to remove his earrings, the centre-forward preferred to simply apply significant amounts of sticky tape to ensure his jewellery presented no scratching hazard to opposition players.

Dirk grew up on Germany's western border, in Aachen, and began playing for a local side before moving to FC Koln, and then on to Belgium where he featured for Lierse and then Molenbeek, before moving back to Germany to Energie Cottbus in 1997.

Alex McLeish secured his services in 1999, and he made his debut at Easter Road against Motherwell – interestingly the other Scottish side he would play for. Again, he proved an instant hit, scoring twice against former Hibs hero Andy Goram in the Motherwell goal in a 2-2 draw.

Dirk, despite his spectacular start, was a sporadic goal-scorer rather than prolific, but his wholehearted commitment to the cause ensured he remained popular during his time at Easter Road.

He was transferred to Brighton and Hove Albion in 2001, before he moved back to Scotland to play for Motherwell. He left the Lanarkshire club in 2003. He then moved on to Japan for a season, before returning to Germany where he played well into his 40s with spells at SSV Jahn Regensberg, Borussia Freialdenhoven and finally Alemannia Bourheim.

At the time of writing, Lehmann was coaching with Sportfreunde Duren in Germany.

GUESS WHO?

There's been a bit of a mix-up with the latest Hibernian photoshoot. See if you can help us sort things out and identify these Hibernian head shots. Answers on p58.

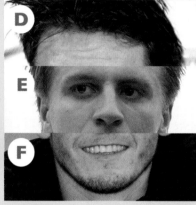

A	
B	
C	

D	
E	
F	

G	
H	
I	

WORD FRENZY

Yet another mix-up! See if you can sort out the confusion and decipher these players' names. Answers on p58.

1. I'm Arty Noble
2. Glad Hind Nanny
3. Con Man Jigs Sum
4. Ugh! Mad Cyclone
5. Fears Verify
6. Barmy Interval
7. Novel Witnesses
8. Giddy Vara
9. Haul on Plan
10. Unclear Calm

HIBERNIAN WORDSEARCH

Find the surnames of ten Hibernian football gaffers. Answers on p58.

```
D  F  W  A  H  S  N  V  W  M  P
N  N  K  B  J  J  C  V  K  M  W
O  S  T  E  I  N  T  Y  L  I  B
M  D  D  F  H  L  C  L  M  L  J
R  Y  R  C  E  P  U  F  S  L  Y
O  T  L  N  O  B  M  B  Y  E  A
C  Q  N  K  N  L  B  K  L  R  R
Y  O  W  R  N  U  L  X  D  X  B
N  Z  U  R  T  A  M  I  C  K  W
P  T  L  S  K  P  H  N  N  C  O
D  L  D  Y  T  M  M  S  K  S  M
```

COLLINS	SHANKLY
LENNON	SHAW
MILLER	STEIN
MOWBRAY	STUBBS
ORMOND	TURNBULL

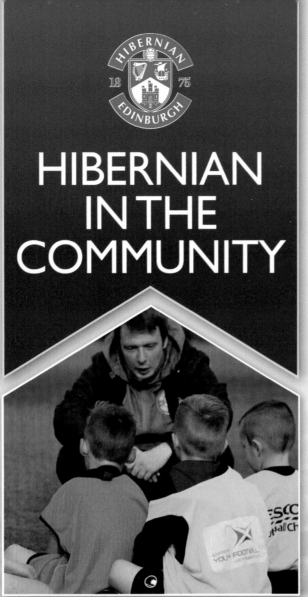

HIBERNIAN IN THE COMMUNITY

The Hibernian Community Foundation has continued with its excellent work, and a particular focus remains getting as many people playing football in Hibernian colours as possible through our ambitious community football programmes.

Fun, healthy and with bags of learning, the Foundation's courses can cater for anyone keen to get involved in football – from tots just 2 years old right through to the other end of the age scale with walking football.

However, getting youngsters engaged with sport, and football in particular, is a big priority and the foundation offers a range of activity all year

round, and also offers holiday camps during school breaks.

The programmes offer seven-week blocks of structured activity, designed not only to provide healthy activity but also to help youngsters develop their footballing skills, and the range of programmes ensures that they don't become bored and can continue to progress. Activities are centred at the Hibernian Training Centre, Easter Road and in a growing number of other locations.

Full information and booking is available at the Foundation website, hiberniancommunityfoundation.org.uk.

In addition, Hibernian Girls and Ladies continue to enjoy significant success, with the Ladies team this past season winning their League Cup to sit alongside the Scottish Cup won by David Gray and his teammates, and again pushing hard in the league.

Lothian Hibernian, the Special Olympics team for the area, continues to enjoy the support of all at the Club and came runners up to England in a tournament in Scandinavia earlier in the year.

Away from football, the Foundation has continued supporting learners through the Learning Centre run in conjunction with Edinburgh College, and delivering a range of health initiatives and programmes, including Fit Fans in Training.

ANSWERS

CUP QUIZ – p 16

1. 1902
2. Rob Jones
3. Lewis Stevenson
4. Kilmarnock
5. "Benji" – Abdessalam Benjelloun
6. Eddie Turnbull
7. Keith Wright
8. Pat Stanton
9. Celtic
10. Dan McMichael

SPOT THE BALL – p 42

Did you guess which was the real ball?

GUESS WHO – p 54

A	Darren McGregor
B	David Gray
C	Grant Holt
D	James Keatings
E	Jason Cummings
F	John McGinn
G	Jordan Forster
H	Liam Fontaine
I	Neil Lennon

WORD FRENZY – p 54

1. MARTIN BOYLE
2. DANNY HANDLING
3. JASON CUMMINGS
4. DYLAN MCGEOUCH
5. FRASER FYVIE
6. MARVIN BARTLEY
7. LEWIS STEVENSON
8. DAVID GRAY
9. PAUL HANLON
10. CALLUM CRANE

WORDSEARCH – p 55

CONTACTS

HIBERNIAN FOOTBALL CLUB
Easter Road Stadium, 12 Albion Place, Edinburgh, EH7 5QG
Email: club@hibernianfc.co.uk
Tel: 0131 661 2159
Twitter: @HibsOfficial
Facebook: Hibernian Football Club Official
Instagram: HibernianFootballClub
Snapchat: @HibsOfficial
YouTube: Hibs TV

SALES & ADVERTISING
– including matchday and player sponsorships and stadium advertising

Rorie Cowan, Sales Manager
Email: rcowan@hibernianfc.co.uk Tel: 0131 656 7073

Brett McGoldrick, Sponsorship Executive
Email: bmcgoldrick@hibernianfc.co.uk Tel: 0131 656 7079

HOSPITALITY & EVENTS
– including matchday hospitality

Lauren Platt, Sales Manager
Email: lplatt@hibernianfc.co.uk Tel: 0131 656 7075

Lynsey McCathie, Sales & Events Assistant
Email: lmccathie@hibernianfc.co.uk Tel: 0131 656 7077

Natalie Brown, Catering & Events Coordinator
Email: nbrown@hibernianfc.co.uk

TICKET OFFICE
Email: tickets@hibernianfc.co.uk Tel: 0844 844 1875

CLUB STORE
http://hibernian.clubstore.co.uk
Tel: 0131 656 7078
hfcclubshop@justsport-group.com

HIBERNIAN HISTORICAL TRUST
Artefacts and memorabilia: curator@hibshistoricaltrust.org.uk

CLUB HISTORY & HONOURS

HISTORY

- Founded in 1875 by members of the Catholic Young Men's Society attached to St Patrick's Church in Edinburgh's "Little Ireland" – the Cowgate.

- Scottish Cup winners in 1887, and a defeat of Preston North End the same year saw Hibernian crowned "World Club Champions".

- Greatest era – The Famous Five years in the 1950s which secured league championships and saw Hibernian as the first British Club to compete in the European Cup, losing at the semi-final stage.

- A second golden era during the 1970s when "Turnbull's Tornadoes" won silverware and played thrilling football.

- Attempted takeover by Hearts owner Wallace Mercer in 1990 as Hibernian faces financial melt-down.

- Present major shareholder Sir Tom Farmer CBE saves the Club from extinction, and a League Cup win follows shortly after in 1991.

- Stadium redeveloped in 1990s and at the turn of the decade.

- Hibernian wins League Cup in 5-1 win over Kilmarnock in March 2007.

- Club opens Hibernian Training Centre in December 2007.

- Stadium redevelopment completed with opening of new East Stand, summer 2010.

- Scottish Cup won for first time since 1902, under guidance of Alan Stubbs in May 2016.

HONOURS

Scottish League Winners (4)	1902/03, 1947/48, 1950/51, 1951/52
First Division winners (2)	1980/81, 1998/99
Division Two winners (3)	1893/94, 1894/95, 1932/33
Division One runners-up (6)	1896/97, 1946/47, 1949/50, 1952/53, 1973/74, 1974/75
Scottish Cup winners (2)	1887, 1902, 2016
Scottish Cup runners-up (9)	1896, 1914, 1923, 1924, 1947, 1958, 1972, 1979, 2001
Scottish League Cup winners (3)	1972/73, 1991/92, 2006/07
Scottish League Cup runners-up (6)	1950/51, 1968/69, 1974/75, 1985/86, 1993/94, 2003/04
Drybrough Cup winners (2)	1972/73, 1973/74
Summer Cup winners (2)	1941, 1964

WHERE'S SUNSHINE?